MW00941708

Jo's Kitchen

By Elaine Auerbach

ISBN:
978-1540546128:

DEDICATION

This book is dedicated to Josephine Auerbach, to all her family and friends, and to those who love to cook or eat.

ACKNOWLEDGMENTS AND DISCLAIMER

The recipes in this book were collected and copied by Josephine Auerbach and come from a variety of sources, books, magazines, family, friends and, of course, from Jo herself. Some were copied and altered per her taste. If any of the recipes should not have been included, the author apologizes.

CONTENTS

ABOUT THIS BOOK

This was going to be a simple book. As Jo Auerbach's daughter, I would select 25 of my mom's favorite recipes, put them in a book and offer it at an event held in her honor at the temple she attended. It was here my family and I have established a fund in her name to be used for events involving cooking and bringing the community together.

My mom, Josephine Auerbach, loved to cook. Her gravestone is a permanent testament to her passion: It reads: "She loved to cook and cooked to love."

I didn't say she was a cook. I said she loved to cook. In her later years, she lost her sense of smell and with it her sense of taste. But she would cook anyway. The alchemy in the kitchen was magical for her. It lifted her to another world. And no matter the results, the effort was what was important.

After she died, I gathered her folders of recipes together, determined to finish the cookbook she started. It was an impossible undertaking. She had spent countless hours clipping, filing and typing out recipes on an old Underwood typewriter. Many were hand copied. Even more were photocopied. From the looks of it, quantity ruled—not quality. She had recipes in every category, a veritable encyclopedia of recipes. She had done a lot of cross referencing and indexing. The recipes extended into other areas. Under "Beer" she says "See Cosmetics" and for "Coffee" she notes, "See House, clothes, cleaning."

1

Oh, mom!

The recipes included items that sounded like they came from the 1950s and I'm sure they did. "For an elegant appetizer…" begins a recipe that surely took hours to make. There were directions for "Coolers" that sounded as if they belonged on a Southern veranda, not in any place she ever lived: Brooklyn, the Bronx or suburban New Jersey. Many recipes used wine or alcohol, which she rarely drank. Others relied on dried milk or other thrifty products and substitutes. If you didn't have an item, she had a recipe to tell you how to come up with a substitute.

Health was also covered. There was a clip saying coffee is bad for you and another that coffee is good for you, and another that the jury is still out. Same for chocolate. If you were on a low calorie diet, there were recipes for how to fool yourself into thinking you were eating a high calorie treat.

The spectrum of foods was huge—among her many beverage recipes were those for mangoade, Scottish fling (a drink with chocolate and molasses) and various ways to serve iced coffee.

Hints abounded: Bread Tabs – "Use the resealing plastic tabs that come with bread for another job. After the bread is gone, slip the tab under the end of masking tape or wrapping tape as soon as you have pulled a piece off the roll. Then, finding the end of the tape next time will be no problem."

"For a quick bread warmer, place aluminum foil underneath the napkin in the bread basket. It keeps heated bread or rolls warm longer."

"To prevent frozen bread from becoming soggy, insert a heavy paper towel in the bag. Reclose it and let the bread thaw. The towel absorbs moisture so the bread stays fresh and firm."

The truth is most of the recipes and hints are more easily found on the internet today and many, ever so many, I doubt you would make. Do you really want to make "Peccadillo Burritos?" She didn't either. The recipe was pristine.

Easy was not her way. She loved unknown items, such as cardoon, a vegetable that reaches five feet tall. She adored strange combinations such as Brussel sprouts and pecans. She loved the more difficult recipes, especially from the New York Times. And many of those that looked simple were a farce. There were several recipes for varieties of egg pasta that looked easy until you got to the last direction: "Follow directions for egg pasta."

Jo exhibited an overwhelming need to use everything. If there was something left over from one recipe, she wanted to be able to add it to another, a never ending chain. For example, she saved information on thousand-year-old eggs. Just in case. Thousand-year-old eggs are duck eggs that have been cured in potash for about 100 days—used primarily in banquet foods. Your banquet—certainly not mine. Of course, you can always substitute with Emperor's Omelet recipe.

What did I learn? There are 40 ways to make lasagna—all of them right. You can put anything in anything and call it a recipe.

Her collection had a lot of duplication—she even noted that by saying "Duplicate" on many of them. Yet she never took it out. Like a true hoarder, she kept every recipe she ever clipped. If she had lived longer, the plastic bins she used to save her recipes would have fallen on her head and killed her, like in the hoarder television shows. There were four maybe five recipes for the same "Spaghetti Bread" and not a one with as much as a sauce smear on it.

Jo typed recipes on the backs of old forms and papers. She was green before it was cool to be green. She picked up recipes everywhere.

When Jo died, I gathered boxes of her recipes, enough for a 60 volume encyclopedia of anything that ever went into your mouth or had anything to do with a plant, food or food product. I was going to scan them into the computer and put them in a book. I soon realized that would have taken the rest of my life and then some. Plus, I didn't even have all the recipes. I had alphabetized files up to L, then it skipped to R, S, T and again to V, where it ended. Even these had huge gaps as there were files for "Chocolate" but none for "Chicken." I am sure there are several boxes of M, N, O, P, Q still lurking in the closets of my brother and sister-in-law's house, where they will stay until they move. For this reason you will not find many meat recipes and I imagine that chicken was under "Poultry," which has yet to appear.

When I tried to figure out the organization of the recipes, I found numbers such as "Vegetable 12-9-6-5." It meant something to her, but I never completely cracked the code. I knew it involved a vegetable but what was 12-9-6-5? I believe it had something to do with where else you could use this vegetable or perhaps what to do with leftovers. She took the code to the grave with her.

What I do recall is that my mother used her system. If she wanted a recipe for potatoes, she would find some box, look something up, go to another box, look something up again and finally go to a box containing a potato recipe she would then make. By that time, I could have microwaved a three-course meal.

I felt guilty throwing out the huge majority of her collection. It bit into my soul, as if I was tossing more dirt on my mother's grave, burying her deeper and deeper, again and again. I couldn't live with that feeling. So I decided to change my way of thinking, to view myself as a curator rather than as a collector. This gave me the right—no, the duty—to sift through the thousands of pieces of paper, throw out the majority, and put the remainder together in a selection that represented Jo.

So how to select?

I began by selecting the ones that looked used (those with food on them or safely encased in plastic coverings) and the ones I remembered. Many were marked "OK" which I took to mean she tested these and they worked. Some she was famous for. Some just looked like she would have made them. Some were examples of the type of recipes she cooked or were those frequently requested by family and friends.

What you will find in these pages is a mish-mash of recipes and my story of my mom, Jo. For those who knew her, it may not be your story of Jo, but it is a testament to her life, her love and yes, even her cooking.

THE STORY AND RECIPES

From hunger comes a love of food. Jo was the first generation born to an immigrant family. My grandmother, Ray, and my grandfather, Benjamin, had come to the United States from Russia, now Poland, in the early 1900s with the wave of poor Jewish immigrants. They were young and hopeful and knew that anything they faced in the United States would be easier than the pogroms, the army and an uncaring stepmother back in the old country. My grandmother was brought to the United States by her brother, Abraham, who had arrived years earlier. Her own mother, my great-grandmother, had died in childbirth with the youngest sister, Hannah. Ray's new stepmother made no secret that she begrudged every bite the children ate and that they were a burden. As soon as Hannah was old enough to travel alone, Abe and Ray brought her to the United States.

In understanding my mother's love of food, I often look to Maslow's hierarchy of needs. My grandmother and grandfather desired safety—to be far from the Czar and his army. The Czar's army meant a lifetime of forced conscription. If that didn't lead to death, there were the regular pogroms, unchecked rage and attacks directed at the Jewish populations. Safety was all. My grandparent's knowledge that they had escaped Russia and probably an early death made them able to survive in times when they had to move since they couldn't pay the rent or when food was scarce.

For my mother, who was relatively safe, the craving was for shelter and food. She and my father, Abraham or "Al" Auerbach, bought a house in the suburbs of New Jersey when my two brothers and I were very young. My mother stayed there until after my dad died, when it was obvious she could not afford to keep it up on her meager Social Security. They also had a cabin in the woods in the Adirondacks, which Jo was able to keep and remains in the family until this day. Shelter was security and they didn't move.

The need for security was demonstrated daily in Jo's obsession with food. Jo recalled that there was never enough to feed a family of seven: my grandparents, four girls and a one boy. My grandfather was a milkman so milk was available, but often little else. Jo loved a good glass of milk but had memories of drinking warm, unpasteurized milk straight from a cow so she always wanted her milk cold. Grandma Ray did piece work at home, sewing bands into men's hats and she learned to stretch a meal. When my mother grew up and had her own family and enough money to buy groceries, she cooked enough to feed an army.

Blueberry Muffins for 70

Preheat oven to 400ºF.
10 cups all-purpose flour
10 teaspoons baking powder
1 teaspoon salt
2 cups sugar
4 cups buttermilk (or 4 cups milk plus 4 tablespoons lemon juice) (can use 1⅓ cups powdered milk)
8 eggs beaten
1 cup (1 pound) margarine melted
2 pints fresh blueberries, washed and tossed in 8 tablespoons flour
Sugar for sprinkling

Sift flour, baking powder, salt and sugar together. Add milk, eggs, margarine and mix until dry ingredients are dampened. Fold in berries. Spoon into greased muffin pans, filling about ⅔ full. Sprinkle with sugar. Bake 20 to 25 minutes until golden brown.

Can use cut apples, walnuts, dates or top with marmalade (scant teaspoon) before baking.

Grocery shopping was an all-day affair. Jo always took at least one child with her —generally all three of us. We were needed to push the multiple carts. I recall going shopping with her and having two even three carts full to the brim with groceries, all for one week. Unlike most kids who would beg their parents to buy this food or that food, we would say "Do we really need that?" The answer was always "yes" and into the cart it would go.

Jo bought so much that food was always rotting in the cramped refrigerator. She loaded up on every fresh vegetable and fruit the supermarket offered. Most of them she forgot she had and three weeks later we'd toss the batch of rotting unused produce, only to go out the next day and buy more.

I once suggested that we could save money by buying fewer things to throw out. My mother's face clouded over like a sudden thunderstorm and she shot back at me much quicker than lightening, "Don't you ever, ever," she spit out, "tell me not to buy food." That food was her safety belt, her lifeline, her security blanket. I got it.

So food it was, even when the electric bill was unpaid, the phone company called to say our phone would be shut off if we didn't pay the bill this week, or we had to turn the heat way down to make the fuel last the winter. It was no matter to Jo. She had her groceries. She was safe.

Here's one recipe that would help clean out the refrigerator.

Chivetch (So your family doesn't kvetch about vegetables)

Carrots, sliced
Cauliflower
Green beans
Green peppers
Potatoes-diced
Zucchini
Squash
Cabbage
2 large onions
4-5 tomatoes
2 cloves garlic
½ stick margarine or butter
Celery
½ cup white wine
½ cup water
2 tablespoons vinegar
Salt, pepper
½ cup olive oil

Fill a casserole with vegetables: carrots, potatoes, strips of green peppers, celery and other vegetables (feel free to add any). To this add the tomatoes or canned tomato sauce or paste.

Slice the onions and garlic. In a skillet, heat the margarine or butter and sauté onions and garlic until lightly browned. Add white wine, water and vinegar, salt and pepper to taste. Bring mix to a boil. Add the olive oil and bring to simmer. Pour the hot broth, onions and garlic over the vegetables. Cover the casserole tightly and bake in pre-heated 350ºF oven for about an hour, or until most of the liquid has evaporated. Remove from oven and let cool to room temperature. Dish can be served hot, warm, room temperature or cold.

In all fairness, Jo used as many or more groceries than those that rotted. That was because my father, Al, demanded a multi-course meal every night.

My dad also came from immigrant Russian parents and grew up in the bowels of New York's immigrant population. His equally large family, including parents, three boys and three girls, faced the same challenges as my mother's family. Grandpa Hyman was a cigar maker, Grandma Rebecca did what she could to supplement the family income. It wasn't enough.

So, like my mother, food was the foundation of the family for my dad. My parents often fought about money but my father never said to cut back on food. He ate with relish—and several other courses. Each night, our dinner would start with a relish tray filled with pickles, green tomatoes, onion slices and other deli items. My father nibbled on these and salted nuts. The relishes were followed by a soup, then the inevitable half of grapefruit. Next, was a salad filled with every fresh vegetable my mother was able to find in the produce aisle. I still enjoy salads filled with interesting vegetables.

The main course always included a cooked vegetable, meat, poultry or fish, a starch such as potatoes or noodles and bread and rolls.

Here's a weekday evening meal. Weekends were more elaborate.

Relish tray: Pickles, green tomatoes, raw onions, scallions on the table and a bowl of nuts.

Salad: Use every vegetable imaginable and lettuces of all types, cucumbers, turnips, scallions, onions, celery, carrots and tomatoes, snap peas, beets, etc.

Appetizer: Baked Eggplant Slices
1 medium eggplant, about 1 pound
1 tablespoon salt
¾ cup olive oil
Juice of 1 lemon
½ teaspoon dried oregano, crushed
Salt (optional)

With a fork, score the eggplant lengthwise. Cut into slices ¼ inch thick and sprinkle with salt. Drain in colander for an hour, then rinse with water and pat dry with paper towels.

Pan-brown eggplant slices in ¼ cup olive oil. When lightly browned, place on baking sheet and bake at 375ºF until very tender. Remove and allow to cool a bit.

Mix remaining ½ cup olive oil with lemon juice, oregano and pepper. Dress slices with this sauce.

Half Grapefruit: sliced so it is easily removed from the skin, with a maraschino cherry in the middle.

Soup: Not Your Mother's Chicken Soup

4 each bone-in-chicken thighs and drumsticks, skin and visible fat removed.
4 cups chicken broth
2 cups water
5 cloves garlic, minced
2 tablespoons finely-chopped fresh ginger
¼ teaspoon black pepper
3 carrots, sliced
1 large leek, well rinsed, white part and some of the green cut in thin slices
1 large sweet potato (12 ounces) peeled and cut into large chunks
6 cups well-rinsed packed torn spinach
1 large tomato, cut into ½ inch chunks

Place chicken, broth, water, garlic, ginger and pepper in a large pot or Dutch oven. Bring to boil over high heat. Skim off any foam that rises to the surface. Reduce heat to low, cover and simmer 15 minutes, skimming surface as needed.

Stir in carrots, leek, and sweet potato. Cover and simmer 20 minutes or until chicken is cooked through and vegetables are tender.

Add spinach and tomato. Cover, cook 5 minutes or until spinach is wilted and tomato is heated through. Add hot pepper sauce.

Bread or Rolls: 90 Minute Dinner Rolls

2 ½ cups unsifted flour
2 tablespoons sugar
½ teaspoon salt
1 package active dry yeast
½ cup milk
¼ cup water
1 tablespoon margarine

Mix ¾ cup flour, sugar, salt and undissolved yeast. Heat milk, water and margarine until liquids are very warm 120ºF to 130ºF. Margarine need not melt. Gradually add to dry ingredients and beat 2 minutes at medium speed using an electric mixer. Add ¼ cup flour. Beat at high speed 2 minutes. Stir in enough additional flour to make a soft dough. Turn onto floured board and knead 2 to 3 minutes until smooth. Divide dough into 12 equal pieces, shape into balls. Arrange in a greased 8-inch round pan.

On the bottom rack of a cold oven, pour boiling water into a large baking pan to the depth of 1 inch. Place rolls on wire rack over the pan of water. Cover. Close the oven door and let rise 30 minutes. Uncover the rolls and remove the pan of water and rack. Turn the oven to 375ºF. Bake 20 to 25 minutes until lightly browned. Remove from pan and cool slightly on rack before serving.

Potatoes: Zesty Oven Potato Fries

1 tablespoon olive oil
1 teaspoon onion powder
1 teaspoon paprika
¼ teaspoon garlic powder
½ teaspoon salt
¼ teaspoon pepper
4 large baking potatoes (about 2½ pounds.) each cut into 4 wedges
Vegetable cooking spray

Preheat oven to 450ºF.

Combine olive oil, onion powder, paprika, garlic powder salt and pepper in a large bowl, stir well. Add potatoes, tossing to coat thoroughly. Arrange potato wedges in a single layer on a baking sheet coated with cooking spray. Bake 30 minutes or until browned. Serves 6.

Vegetable: Orange Carrots

1 pound carrots, cut into ¼ inch slices
½ teaspoon salt
¾ cup water
½ teaspoon fresh orange peel, grated
1 orange, peeled, cut in bite-size pieces
2 tablespoons butter or margarine, softened
1 tablespoon chopped green onion

In a covered saucepan, cook carrots with salt in water until just tender (10 to 15 minutes). Drain.

Add remaining ingredients, heat; stirring occasionally. Makes 4 servings.

Meats

When my father was at home, meats were generally plain, broiled, and burnt. There were steaks, hamburgers, lamb chops and veal chops. He enjoyed the burnt ends of roasts. I've long wondered if the char broiled meats speeded his demise from cancer years later.

Desserts:

After a full meal, there was dessert: cake, pie or shortcake. My dad routinely followed this with chocolate ice cream, eaten directly out of the half-gallon carton.

An oft-told story was how my dad, Al, and his friend Walter, bought two cartons of ice cream and proceeded to walk each other home while eating it. Since they were not finished when they got to the first apartment, they walked back to the second apartment.

Ice cream was generally eaten plain but my mother made other chocolate treats.

Brown Sugar Fudge

¼ butter or margarine
½ cup brown sugar firmly packed
1 pound confectionary sugar
⅓ cup instant non-fat dry milk
⅓ cup dark corn syrup
1 teaspoon vanilla
⅓ cup chopped nuts

Butter 8-inch square pan.

Melt butter and brown sugar in top of double boiler over boiling water.

Meanwhile, sift the confectionary sugar and nonfat dry milk together and set aside.

Stir corn syrup and vanilla into brown sugar mix over the boiling water.

Stir in sifted dry ingredients, half at a time, stirring each time until it is blended and smooth.

Remove the mixture from the boiling water. Stir in nuts. Turn into pan. Cool, cut into squares. Makes 36 squares of fudge.

Chocolate Fudge Brownie Pie

2 eggs
1 cup sugar
½ cup butter or margarine, melted
½ cup flour
⅓ cup cocoa
¼ teaspoon salt
1 teaspoon vanilla
½ cup chopped nuts (optional)
Ice cream and hot fudge sauce (see next recipe)

Beat eggs in a small mixing bowl. Blend in sugar and melted butter. Combine flour, cocoa and salt; add to butter mix. Stir in vanilla and nuts. Pour into lightly greased 8-inch pie pan. Bake at 350ºF for 25 to 30 minutes or until almost set (pie will not test done). Cool; cut into wedges. Serve topped with ice cream and hot fudge sauce. 6 to 8 servings.

If there was a product on the shelves, Jo tried to make it.

Hot Fudge Sauce

½ cup cocoa
¾ cup sugar
1 small can (5 ounces) evaporated milk
⅓ cup light corn syrup
⅓ cup butter or margarine
1 teaspoon vanilla

Combine sugar and cocoa in a small saucepan; blend in evaporated milk and corn syrup. Cook over medium heat, stirring constantly until mix boils. Boil and stir for 1 minutes. Remove from heat, stir in butter and vanilla.

Chocolate-Filled Bon Bon cookies

1 cup butter
½ cup confectioners' sugar
1 teaspoon vanilla extract
2¼ cups flour
½ teaspoon salt
Hershey's Kisses ™

Cream butter and sugar.
Add vanilla extract.
Add flour and salt. Mix until blended.
Wrap 2 teaspoons dough evenly around each Hershey's Kisses™
Bake at 350ºF for 10 to 12 minutes on parchment paper.
Makes about 30 cookies.

She tried candies. I remember eating a variety of gooey confections. Here's two I enjoyed that can be used for holidays.

Peppermint Truffles.

½ pound bittersweet chocolate
6 tablespoons butter
⅓ cup evaporated milk
2 tablespoons dark rum
1 pound white chocolate
½ pound candy canes or peppermint candy, crushed

Melt bittersweet chocolate in top of double boiler over hot water or in microwave oven. Let cool. Melt butter, cool. Pour cooled butter into the bowl of an electric mixer and slowly add evaporated milk. Add cooled chocolate and rum. Cover and refrigerate until mix sets, about 1 hour. Form into small balls, using small end of melon baller or rolling with your hands. Freeze balls until firm. Once frozen, balls may be put into an airtight container and kept frozen until ready to be dipped.

Melt white chocolate in small bowl over hot water or in microwave. Crush candy canes and spread on piece of waxed paper. Taking about 10 truffles from the freezer at a time, dip balls into white chocolate, lift out with fork, let excess run off, then drop onto crushed peppermint candy and roll to cover. Let harden. Store in airtight container in single layers, keep in cool place. Makes about 60 truffles.

Chocolate Mint Hearts, Chocolate Layers

1 12 ounces package semi-sweet chocolate chips, divided.
4 measuring tablespoons of shortening, divided.

Fondant Filling:
6 tablespoons butter
½ cup light corn syrup
4½ cups sifted confectionery sugar, divided
1 teaspoon peppermint extract
Red food coloring

Chocolate Bottom Layer:

Combine over hot (not boiling) water, 1 cup semi-sweet chocolate chips morsels and 2 tablespoons shortening. Heat until morsels melt and mix is smooth. Spread evenly with back of spoon in aluminum foil-lined 15 by 10 by 1 inch pan. Chill in refrigerator until firm (about 20 minutes). Carefully invert onto waxed paper lined cookie sheet. Gently peel off foil. Return to refrigerator.

Fondant Filling:

In a large saucepan, combine butter, corn syrup and half the confectionery sugar. Bring to full boil, stirring constantly over medium-low heat. Add remainder of the confectionery sugar, peppermint extract and desired amount of food coloring. Stir vigorously until well-blended (about 2-3 minutes). Remove from heat. Pour fondant onto greased cookie sheet. Cool just enough to handle (5 minutes). Knead until soft, 2 to 3 minutes. Roll out fondant to ⅛ inch thick between two pieces of plastic wrap. Carefully place on top of bottom chocolate layer. Remove second sheet of plastic wrap. Chill 15 minutes. Top with chocolate top layer.

Chocolate Top Layer:

Prepare the same as for the chocolate bottom layer. Spread melted chocolate evenly over fondant filling. Chill 15 to 20 minutes. Cut out 24 hearts with 2 inch heart-shaped cookie cutter. Chill until ready to serve. Yields 24 hearts.

My parents married August 19, 1939. The new couple lived with Grandma Ray, as did everyone else. The two-story building in the Bronx housed Grandma Ray and Grandpa Ben, my aunts Bertha, Miriam, Evelyn and Uncle Sheldon as well as my mother. As spouses were added, they moved in or moved nearby. My older brother Karl (born 1943) and I (born 1945) spent our first years on the flowered linoleum of the living room, playing with my cousins, Abe, and then Robert. When my younger brother Michael (born 1947) came along, my parents had managed to save, borrow and beg enough money to buy a brick Cape Cod home in northern New Jersey. With its farmlands and open lots to play in, Saddle Brook (then called Saddle River Township) seemed a million miles away from New York, although a bus could get my grandmother to our house in half an hour, where I would sometimes find her in the kitchen when I came home from school.

Jo's sister Miriam added some recipes to the favorites.

Chocolate Chip Pudding Cookies

2 ½ cups unsifted flour
1 teaspoon baking soda
1 cup butter or margarine softened (2 quarters)
¼ cup granulated sugar
¾ cup firmly packed brown sugar
1 small size vanilla instant pudding (chocolate instant may be substituted)
1 teaspoon vanilla
2 eggs
1 package (12 ounces) chocolate chips
1 cup chopped nuts (optional)

Mix flour with baking soda.

Combine margarine (or butter), sugars, vanilla and pudding mix in a large bowl, beat until smooth and creamy, beat in eggs. Gradually add flour mix, then stir in chips and nuts. Batter will be stiff. Drop by rounded teaspoonful onto ungreased cookie sheet about 2 inches apart. Bake at 375ºF for 8 to10 minutes. Makes about 7 dozen.

Aunt Miriam's Sugar Cookies

1 cup shortening or butter
1½ cups sugar
4 egg yolks
8 tablespoons milk
5 cups flour
2 teaspoons baking powder
1 teaspoon salt
1 teaspoon vanilla extract

Cream shortening, sugar, egg yolks and vanilla until light and fluffy. Sift flour, baking powder and salt three times. Add milk then sifted dry ingredients to shortening mix. Add a little at a time until all ingredients are blended, lowering the mixer speed to slow at the end. Roll on floured board with floured rolling pin. Cut with cookie cutters and decorate as desired. Bake at 350ºF for 10 minutes.

My father spent World War II as 4F but doing his part by working for an electronics company on radios used for wartime. After the war, he opened a small radio repair shop in the New York City borough of the Bronx. When they moved to New Jersey, he extended his reach to the new televisions that were just becoming available. His first AA Television repair store was a tiny affair in Rochelle Park, New Jersey. My mother kept the store open, waited on customers and worked on huge piles of ironing while we three small children played underfoot.

When the business grew, he moved it to our hometown of Saddle Brook, New Jersey and expanded into television sales as well as service. Until the mid-1950s when the big box stores came into being, it made a sparse but survivable living for our family. Enough so my parents could dream of a future. They juggled the work, with my father going on house calls (repairmen came to your house then) and my mother in the store. Then he'd return and she would head home to make dinner. Generally, it was the typical multi-course meal. Sometimes she would add a flourish, as when she made radishes into "coin jacks" or flowers.

Radish Coin Jacks

Slice radishes crosswise into ⅛ inch coin slices.

Make a cut from center of each coin slice to outer edge.

Bend two radish slices slightly to open the cuts. Slide cuts into each other so that they interlock at right angles.

Radish Chrysanthemums

Choose as round a radish as possible. Using a sharp paring knife trim off leaves and tips.

Make very thin parallel cuts into the radish, as close together as possible and to ⅛ inch of stem.

Turn radish 90 degrees to make an equal number of parallel cuts perpendicular to the first. Soak in ice water to open fully.

Insert one end of a toothpick into the bottom of the radish. Insert opposite end into top of a scallion to make the stem.

Al enjoyed the outdoors. The story I was told was that he was a twin, but his twin was dead at birth. Al lived but was frail. To build him up, his parents sent him to the country, Newburgh, New York, where he learned to love the outdoors. This love carried over and in his youth he discovered Lake George, the queen of the Adirondack lakes in upstate New York. My parents went there on their honeymoon, camping on a lake island in a pup tent. My mother took to it and once my brothers and I came along, they took us there camping, even as infants. Often we also took my cousin, Abe, two years older than me. So there were four children and two adults.

Vacations were all the same—two weeks camping at Lake George. For years we camped at Hearthstone Point, which was close to the honkytonk world of Lake George Village, New York, but far enough away so going to play an arcade game was a rare treat.

Cooking did not stop when we went camping. Despite the fact that it was more difficult since it was done over a Coleman propane gas stove or in the open fireplace, my mother created outstanding meals with a typical overabundance of food.

Breakfasts were especially delicious and generally included fruit, eggs, pancakes or French toast, or something special.

Apple Fritters

4 medium-sized tart cooking apples, cored and peeled
Sugar
½ teaspoon nutmeg
2 tablespoon lemon juice
Oil for deep frying
1 cup all-purpose flour
½ teaspoon salt
1 cup beer

Slice apples in ½ inch rings. Sprinkle with sugar and the nutmeg and pour lemon juice over the top. Let stand one hour. Heat oil in heavy 8 inch or 9 inch saucepan or Dutch oven to 380ºF on frying thermometer. Mix flour, salt and ½ cup beer. Add remaining beer, beating until smooth. Dip apple slices in batter and fry a few at a time until well-browned and puffy. Drain on absorbent paper and sprinkle with more sugar.

Preparations for the annual trip to the lake were arduous and took days since we had to take anything and everything we might possibly need.

We had a huge 16 feet by 12 feet green canvas army tent, complete with heavy wooden poles and a 2 inches by 4 inches rafter that spanned the length. There were canvas army cots, heavy army surplus sleeping bags, pillows, blankets. My father built two wooden boxes, each about 16 inches high and 4 feet by 4 feet square. Each box had a hinged door that dropped down to reveal two compartments on each side, making a total of eight shelves. These heavy boxes went on top of the old green station wagon. Each person, child and adult, had a compartment. We packed our things inside, along with multiple pots, pans, bowls, utensils, dishes, camping stove, Coleman lantern, hatchets to cut wood, spices, oil, canned goods and assorted gadgets we might need.

Packing typically continued until the wee hours of the morning when we were scheduled to leave in order to avoid the traffic. Finally, at about 2 am, my father would yell "Everybody into the car!" My mother and one chosen child would sit in the front seat, and the other three or four kids in the back seat.

Some years, we would pack the car so tightly that we had to put the back seat of the station wagon down to fit all the luggage. Then the back seat kids would be forced to lie spread out on the top of the gear, almost touching the roof of the car, where we could sleep the journey away or wave our feet to passing cars. Car seats and seat belts had yet to be invented.

When I was about 9 years old, about 1954, my father purchased a canvas rowboat to which he attached a 15 horsepower motor. We all learned to water ski behind this and it was the entry to meeting new friends, including one family from Canada, the Baylin's, who became like family and we forged a lifetime bond. A side benefit of the boat was that we could pack it with items, leaving more room to actually sit in the car.

With the addition of a boat, we tried our hand at fishing. The only thing we caught were sunfish, which my mother dutifully cooked for us. She used a standard fish recipe.

Crispy Flounder

2 tablespoons skim milk
1 tablespoon low-sodium soy sauce
¼ teaspoon garlic powder
1 egg white, lightly beaten
4 (4 ounces) skinned flounder fillets
⅓ cup fine dry breadcrumbs
¼ cup grated Parmesan cheese
1 teaspoon vegetable oil, divided
Lemon wedges

Combine skim milk, soy sauce, garlic powder and beaten egg white in a large shallow dish; stir well. Add fish, turning to coat. Marinate in refrigerator (or ice box when camping) for 15 minutes, turning the fish once. Remove the fish from the marinade and discard the marinade.

Combine bread crumbs and cheese in a large zip-top plastic bag. Add fish fillets, seal bag and shake to coat. Remove fish from bag, discard remaining bread crumb mix.

Heat ½ teaspoon oil in a large nonstick skillet over medium heat until hot. Add 2 pieces of fish and cook 2½ minutes on each side or until fish flakes easily with a fork.

Place cooked fillet on a serving platter. Repeat the procedure with the remaining oil and fish. Serve garnished with lemon wedges. Serves 4.

Sometime in the early 1950s we arrived at Hearthstone Point to find it full. This was in the days before it was necessary to reserve a camping spot. We decided to take an island campground, which was still available. We had the boat. The problem was that it was about to storm. We loaded the tent and part of our gear in the tiny open boat. The plan was for my father to take me and the gear to the island, where I would wait while he returned for more gear and people.

If it was nice weather, the plan would have worked. Instead, it started to pour and thunder as we made our way the few miles to the island site. Working feverishly, the two of us worked to set up the tent so we could keep things dry. Instead, the rain and storm were so fierce we couldn't fight the wind and it was too dangerous to go back on the water.

My memory of the night is dim since I was more than terrified when lightening hit the metal rod sticking out of our tent pole, which I was holding. I felt a jolt, dropped the pole and forever after believed I was hit by lightning. My father and I spent the night under the campground picnic table. In the morning, in the calm after the storm, he returned to shore to get the remainder of the group, who had spent the night in the car.

The gear we had brought to the island on the first trip was soaked and covered with mud. We spent hours cleaning it up and then setting up camp. Meanwhile, my mother cooked food to reward and warm us.

Savory Tomato Soup

2 teaspoons olive oil
½ cup red pepper
½ cup yellow pepper
½ cup red onion
½ cup carrots
½ cup celery
1 cup savory cabbage (shredded)
2 cups diced tomatoes
1 tablespoon minced garlic
¼ cup balsamic vinegar
2 teaspoons dried basil
1 teaspoon tarragon
½ teaspoon salt
1 bay leaf
1-5 ounces can tomato paste
4 cups stock or water
1 cups tomato juice
1 cup broccoli florets
1 cup cooked pasted (fusilli or whatever is available)
Croutons
Parmesan cheese

In a large soup pot, sauté in the olive oil on medium heat, red pepper, yellow pepper, red onion, carrot and celery. Add shredded savory cabbage, diced tomato, minced garlic. Cook until cabbage softens, about 6 to 8 minutes. Then add, balsamic vinegar, dried basil, tarragon, salt, bay leaf, tomato paste, stock or water, tomato juice. Simmer for 15 minutes. Add bite-sized broccoli florets, cooked fusilli or other pasta. Serve with croutons and grated parmesan cheese.

The next year when we went to Lake George, we again found Hearthstone Point filled with campers and were advised that there was a second campground further north. This might have been the year my mother drove our big van into the ditch. My parents had purchased a GMC van to use for the family, for hauling and for business. We were probably searching for an empty campsite when she slipped off the one lane road of the campsite and landed in the culvert.

Once the van was pulled out, we headed north to Roger's Rock Campgrounds, located on the most northern part of the lake, near historic Fort Ticonderoga.

It was at Roger's Rock Campgrounds that we met the Baylin family, comprised of Ben, Martha and their daughters, Neomi and Jackie. On many nights, we'd sit under our huge tarp at the big wooden campground picnic table and, with the light of the Coleman lantern swarming with bugs above us, we'd spend the evening playing cards and eating snacks my mother kept coming.

Although I can't recall any recipe in particular, these meatballs would be typical since they were filling, easily made and delicious.

Tiny Meatballs

1 pound lean ground round
¼ teaspoon garlic powder
1 medium onion, finely chopped
1 cup skim milk
½ teaspoon black pepper
¼ cup wheat germ
1 teaspoon dry mustard
1 tablespoon vegetable oil

Mix all ingredients and form into 30 tiny meatballs. Heat oil in skillet and brown meatballs on all sides. Pour off fat. May be served with sweet and sour sauce.

The love affair with Lake George continued and in 1958 my parents purchased a one room log cabin located in Silver Bay, New York, a tiny community at the bottom of Five Mile Mountain, which separated the northern and southern parts of the lake. North and south were different worlds. In the south was Lake George Village, arcades, miniature golf courses, motels with names like "Blue Lagoon," boats and tour boats, fast-food joints and Frankenstein's House of Horrors. The north was scarcely populated, quiet, one store and the Silver Bay Association, which wascalled the "Summer Home of the YMCA" and offered a variety of programs for adults and children. It was heaven for children.

The house was an authentic log cabin, with logs in the front and Adirondack, or "pig pen" siding as it was called, on the other three sides. The one room included a beautiful stone fireplace in the middle, two beds on one end and room for a table on the other end. There was a Murphy bed in the wall that could come down in the dining area. The kitchen was a tiny alcove off the dining area. The kitchen was only about 10 feet long, and two feet wide. It opened up to the main room but could be hidden with a panel that pulled up out of the floor. There was a toilet and sink, cold water only, a small screened-in porch and a cold water shower outside behind a storage shed.

The house had been built and owned by the Mr. and Mrs. Mosher, a couple that vacationed there for years. After her husband died, Mrs. Mosher decided to sell. We could feel her love for the place and felt she understood we would love it as much as she did.

But with a family of five, plus visiting cousins, the house needed changes. We began by adding hot water, an indoor shower and building an addition that included two bedrooms and an upstairs room with a small kitchen and tiny bath. My parents dreamed of retiring to the cabin. They planned that during the summer, they would move upstairs to the apartment and rent the bottom out for income.

The kitchen in the cabin was far too small for my mother's cooking, so little by little my mother began taking over the dining area. Pots hung down in the entrance way on a huge round wrought iron pot holder, dishes were next to the window area, wooden shelves held canned and dry goods. Soon half the house was kitchen.

The changes took work as did maintenance. My father believed in child labor—any child. We were conscripted into building, digging, sanding, staining, raking and picking up twigs. We were required to pick up large branches and twigs from the area around the house and pile them for firewood.

Another typical task was moving streams. The house stood at the top of an embankment. At the bottom was a stream that was cutting into the hill. My father worried it would jeopardize the house so he had us move boulders in the stream in an attempt to change its course. We typically worked an eight-hour day and at about 5 pm we were permitted to go swimming or my father would take us water skiing.

All this built up appetites. During the day my mother, who was not a swimmer and never shirked work, would clean, organize and cook.

Breakfast was a hearty affair. Lunch brought sandwiches and salads. Dinner was the multi-course affair it always was, topped off by plenty of snacks and desserts. Since time was tight she often used shortcuts. A constant stream of food and more food flowed from the tight quarters.

Apple Nut Ring

2 -8 ounces cans refrigerated buttermilk biscuits
¾ cup sugar
1 tablespoon cinnamon
¼ cup butter
2 medium apples
⅓ cup chopped nuts
¼ cup raisins (optional)

Separate biscuits into 20 pieces. Combine sugar and cinnamon. Dip biscuits into melted butter then roll in the sugar mix. Arrange biscuits around the outer edge of a deep dish baking pan, using a total of 15 pieces, overlap the remaining 5 biscuits in the center. Peel, core and slice apples into thin slices. Place an apple slice between each biscuit and place apple slices all around the outer edge of deep dish baker. Mix nuts and raisins with remaining sugar mixture and pour over the biscuits. Bake at 400ºF for 25 to 30 minutes.

Pancakes (or Waffles)

4 cups unbleached all-purpose flour (or 1 cup whole wheat flour and 3 cups all-purpose flour)
3 tablespoons sugar
1 tablespoon baking powder
1 teaspoon salt
½ teaspoon baking soda
4 eggs
1 quart buttermilk (or 1 quart sweet milk to which you've added 1 tablespoon vinegar or lemon juice and let stand for 5 minutes).

Preheat skillet or waffle iron.

Blend with a wire whisk in a large mixing bowl the flour, sugar, baking powder, salt and baking soda.

In a smaller bowl beat the eggs and buttermilk together until light and fluffy. Blend wet ingredients into dry, don't over mix. Grease pan and pour batter. Cook 2 to 4 minutes, turning when bubbles appear.

Raspberry Sauce (for pancakes, ice cream, etc.)

1 quart fresh raspberries
1 cup sugar
2 tablespoons all-purpose flour
2 tablespoons molasses

In a saucepan over medium heat, combine ingredients. Cook until thickened, about 5 minutes. Serve over pancakes, waffles, blintzes or ice cream.

Apple Pancakes

¼ cup plus 1 tablespoon whole wheat flour
4 teaspoons instant dry milk powder
½ teaspoon baking powder
1 small apple, cored and grated
¼ cup water

Sift flour, milk powder and baking powder together into a bowl. Stir in apple and water. Ladle about 2 tablespoons per pancake onto preheated nonstick griddle. Cook until golden, turning once.
Makes 6 pancakes.

Some of my best memories were seeing lines of little round blintz shells lined up on the table, ready for filling. I loved the fruit fillings.

Cheese Blintzes and Variations

Batter
1 cup sifted all-purpose flour
1 teaspoon salt
4 eggs, well beaten
1 cup milk or 1 cup water

Filling
1½ cups dry cottage cheese
1 or 2 egg yolks, beaten
1 tablespoon melted butter
Salt, sugar and cinnamon to taste

Batter: Sift flour and salt. Mix eggs with liquid. Stir in flour. Mix until smooth to form thin batter. On a hot lightly greased 6-inch skillet, pour enough batter to form a very thin cake, tilting the pan from side to side so the batter spreads evenly. Cook over a low heat on one side only until the top of the cake is dry and blistered. Turn out on clean cloth, cooked side up. Allow to cool. Repeat until all batter is used.

Filling: Mix cheese with egg yolks and butter and with salt, sugar and cinnamon to taste. Place a tablespoon of mixture in center of each cake. Fold edges over to form envelope. Blintzes may be prepared and filled in advance and kept in refrigerator until ready to fry. Just before serving, fry in butter until brown on both sides or bake in a moderate oven. Serve hot with sour cream or with sugar and cinnamon mixture.

Yield: about 10 blintzes.

Variations:

Apple blintzes: Mix 2 cups peeled and cored chopped apples, 1½ tablespoons ground almonds, 1 egg white, powdered sugar and cinnamon to taste. Proceed as for cheese blintzes. Serve with sugar and cinnamon mixture.

Cherry blintzes: Mix 1 cup drained, pitted canned cherries, dash of cinnamon, 1 tablespoon flour and sugar to taste. Proceed as for cheese blintzes. Serve with sour cream or with cinnamon and sugar.

Blueberry blintzes: Substitute blueberries for cherries.

Meat blintzes: Combine 2 cups fine ground or chopped lean, cooked meat, 1 egg, ½ teaspoon salt, ¼ teaspoon pepper and 2 tablespoons of soup stock. Mix thoroughly. Use as filling instead of cheese. Use water instead of milk in batter for blintzes.

Other variations: Substitute chopped, seasoned leftover meat, kasha, poppy seed filling or preserves for cheese filling.

Not surprising, weight was a problem. Jo was always on a diet. Her recipes were often three types: diet, regular, and extra luscious. For example, here are three versions of brownies.

Brownies

½ cup butter, melted
1 cup sugar
½ cup brown sugar
½ cup unsweetened cocoa
2 eggs
½ cup flour
1 teaspoon baking powder
1 teaspoon vanilla
½ cup chopped nuts (pecans or walnuts)

Heat oven to 350ºF.

In mixing bowl, beat butter, sugars and cocoa until well-blended.

Beat in eggs, one at a time.

In small bowl, mix flour and baking powder, stir into butter/sugar/cocoa mix.

Pour into greased or foil-lined 8-inch square cake pan.

Bake 25 to 30 minutes or until cake tester or toothpick inserted in center comes out clean.

Cool completely. Cut into 2 inch squares.

Diet Brownies

¼ plus 2 tablespoons margarine, melted
⅓ cup unsweetened cocoa powder
⅓ cup all-purpose flour
¼ cup chopped walnuts
½ teaspoon baking powder
⅛ teaspoon salt
2 eggs
⅓ cup sugar
1 teaspoon Sweet'n Low ™ granulated sugar substitute
1 teaspoon vanilla extract
¼ teaspoon chocolate extract

In small bowl, combine margarine and cocoa. Set aside. In another small bowl, stir together flour, walnuts, baking powder and salt.

Preheat oven to 350ºF.

Spray 8-inch square baking pan with non-stick cooking spray. In medium bowl, beat eggs. Beat in sugar and Sweet'n Low™. Beat in vanilla and chocolate extracts. Beat in cocoa mix.

With rubber spatula or wooden spoon, gently fold in flour mix. Do not beat. Pour into pan. Bake 15 minutes or until edges begin to brown. Cool completely on rack before cutting.

Yields 16 servings. 100 calories per serving.

Rocky Road Brownies

4 squares unsweetened chocolate
¾ cup margarine or butter
2 cups sugar
4 eggs
1 teaspoon vanilla
1 cup all-purpose flour
2 cups miniature marshmallows
1 cup chocolate chips
1 cup coarsely chopped nuts

Preheat oven to 350ºF. Heat chocolate and margarine in microwaveable bowl on high for 2 minutes or until margarine is melted. (Or heat in 1 quart saucepan over very low heat, stirring constantly until chocolate is melted.) Stir until chocolate is completed melted. Stir in sugar until well-blended. Beat in eggs and vanilla. Stir in flour until well-mixed. Spread in greased 13 inch by 9 inch pan. Bake for 35 minutes. Immediately sprinkle marshmallows, then chocolate chips and nuts over brownies. Continue to bake 3 to 5 minutes, until toppings begin to melt together. Cool in pan, cut into squares. Yields 24 brownies.

Jo was always on the lookout for healthier alternatives. Here are two oatmeal cookie recipes. One is healthier than the other but when all is said and done, they are still cookies.

Oatmeal Raisin Cookies

1½ cup oatmeal (regular or quick cooking)
1 cup all-purpose flour
½ teaspoon baking soda
¼ teaspoon ground cinnamon
Whites of 2 large eggs
1 cup packed brown sugar
½ cup skim milk
⅓ cup vegetable oil
1 teaspoon vanilla extract
1 cup raisins

Pre-heat oven to 375ºF. Mix oats, flour, baking soda and cinnamon in a large bowl. Lightly beat egg whites in medium sized bowl. Stir in sugar, milk, oil and vanilla, then raisins. Add to flour mixture, mix well. Drop batter a teaspoon at a time onto a lightly greased baking sheet. Bake about 12 minutes for chewy, soft cookies; about 15 minutes for crispy cookies. Transfer cookies to wire rack to cool. Makes about 3 dozen.

Whole Wheat Oatmeal Cookies

1 cup whole wheat flour
1 teaspoon ground cinnamon
1 teaspoon baking powder
½ teaspoon salt
1 cup packed light brown sugar
¼ cup unsweetened applesauce
2 egg whites
2 tablespoons margarine
1½ teaspoon vanilla
1⅓ cups uncooked quick oats
½ cup raisins

Preheat oven to 375ºF. Lightly spray cookie sheets with nonstick cooking spray.

Combine flour, cinnamon, baking powder, baking soda and salt in medium bowl. Mix well.

Combine brown sugar, applesauce, egg whites, margarine and vanilla in a large bowl. Mix well until small crumbs form. Add flour mixture, mix well. Fold in oats and raisins.

Drop by rounded teaspoons onto prepared cookie sheets, 2 inches apart. Bake 10 to 12 minutes until golden brown. Cool on wire racks. Makes about 40 cookies.

She loved to experiment with vegetables in unfamiliar places.

Zucchini Muffins

2 cups sifted all-purpose flour
2 teaspoons baking powder
Low cholesterol egg substitute equivalent to 2 large eggs
⅓ cup polyunsaturated oil
½ cup sugar
1 teaspoon ground cinnamon
½ teaspoon allspice
1/8 teaspoon cloves
1 teaspoon grated orange rind
1½ cups finely grated zucchini
Vegetable cooking spray

Stir flour, baking powder and set aside.

In a large bowl, beat egg substitute, oil, sugar, cinnamon, allspice, cloves and orange rind. Stir in zucchini and flour mix until well blended.

Spray 12 muffin cups with vegetable cooking spray. Spoon batter into muffin cups.

Bake in preheated 450ºF oven for 15 to 20 minutes, until toothpick inserted comes out clean. Serve warm.

In fact, she loved to experiment with everything—even this tricky dessert.

Baked Alaska

1 box chocolate cake mix
3 egg whites
4 tablespoons sugar
½ cup raspberry jam, melted and cooled slightly
1 pint vanilla ice cream softened

Prepare a single layer 9-inch chocolate cake according to package instructions. Bake and cool completely.

For meringue, beat egg whites until stiff peaks form. Carefully fold in sugar and set aside.

Place cake on ovenproof plate. Spread jam evenly over the cake. Cover with ice cream. Immediately spread meringue mix over top, covering the ice cream completely.

Bake at 350ºF for 2 to 3 minutes until meringue turns light brown. Serve immediately.

Back at home in Saddle Brook, the food flowed freely all year but holidays brought special dishes. My parents weren't traditionally religious. This was partly because of their free-thinking views, partly because my dad had gotten an infection as an infant when a mohel, the ritual circumciser, used dirty instruments, and partly because there were few Jews in our predominantly Catholic town at this time. Yet, my mother cooked Jewish from habit and, if not with prayer, the Jewish holidays were celebrated with that old-time religion: food.

These were favorites.

Carrot-Meat Tzimmas

Recipe is for 5 to 6 persons, calculating ½ pound meat per person.
2 ½ pounds brisket, all fat removed
1 medium-sized onion
1 stalk celery
1 quart fruit juice (apple is good)
1 tablespoon salt
½ teaspoon white pepper
2 cups medium dried prunes
5 carrots, scraped
1 can sweet potatoes-15 ounces or more
½ pound dried apricots
½ cup raisins
1-20 ounces can crushed pineapple
2 tablespoons flour
½ cup lemon juice
⅓ cups brown sugar
Place meat, onion, celery, juice, salt and pepper in a 4-quart saucepan. Bring to boil, cover, and simmer until tender. Remove onion and celery. Add prunes, carrots, sweet potatoes, apricots and raisins. Cook until vegetables are tender. Strain, remove excess fat from liquid. Reserve 2 cups liquid.

Place meat, fruits and vegetables in a well-greased 3-quart oven-proof glass casserole.

In a separate saucepan, mix flour and sugar together, add a few spoonful's of cold water and stir to a paste. Stir in reserved liquid. Bring to a boil and cook and stir until thickened. Pour sauce over meat mixture, cover casserole and bake at 350ºF for 50 minutes. Uncover and bake 10 minutes longer.

Fruit Noodle Pudding

8 ounces wide egg noodles
2 tablespoons cinnamon
2 eggs
½ cup raisins (white)
¼ pound butter or margarine, melted
1 tablespoon lemon juice
½ cup sugar
2 apples, peeled, cored and sliced

Cook noodles 8 minutes. Drain.

Butter bottom of a 9-inch square pan. Put apples and raisins on bottom.

Stir noodles with eggs, sugar, lemon and butter. Cover the apples and raisins.

Top with cinnamon. Bake at 350ºF for 1 hour.

Can be prepared ahead of time and reheated. Do not freeze.

Here's a variation.

Noodle Kugel

¼ cup butter, melted (or oil)
¾ cup dark brown sugar
1 cup chopped pecans
1 – 16 ounces package of medium noodles
4 eggs, beaten (or Egg-Beaters™)
½ teaspoon cinnamon
⅔ cup sugar
1 cup sour cream (or use yogurt)
1-3 ounces package of cream cheese, softened (or use farmer cheese)

Spray a Bundt pan with non-stick spray. Pour ¼ cup melted butter into the pan. Sprinkle brown sugar evenly over the butter. Sprinkle nuts over brown sugar. Cook noodles as directed on the package and drain. In a large bowl, mix together eggs, cinnamon, sugar, sour cream and cream cheese. Add noodles and mix thoroughly. Pour into the Bundt pan and bake in a 250ºF oven for 1 hour or until golden brown. Remove from oven, invert onto plate. Serve warm or at room temperature.

One story that is famous in our family is "The day mom put her finger in the mixer."

She was baking for Rosh Hashanah, the Jewish New Year. Tradition calls for dipping apples in honey and using honey in recipes to represent a sweet new year. Jo was in the kitchen when we heard a very controlled plaintive voice call "Help! Help!" She had put her finger in the beaters while trying to take a short cut to scraping the bowl. Don't ask.

We called the ambulance (no 911 in those days), held her head so she wouldn't pass out and plied her with whiskey so she wouldn't hurt too much. The emergency team finally came, cut the beaters and whisked her off to the hospital. This was the recipe she was making.

Honey Cake

2 tablespoons oil
1 cup sugar
3 eggs
1 cup cold strong coffee
1 cup liquid honey
3 cups sifted cake flour
2 teaspoons double acting baking powder
1 teaspoon baking soda
1 teaspoon cinnamon
½ teaspoon ground ginger
½ teaspoon ground nutmeg

Beat oil, sugar and eggs until light and thick. Combine coffee and honey. Sift dry ingredients together. Add to batter alternating with coffee-honey mixture. Pour into greased and floured plan and bake at 325ºF about 70 minutes, until toothpick inserted in the center comes out clean. Remove from pan and place on a wire rack to cool.

Of course she made challah, the traditional Jewish braided bread, as well as many other yeast breads. The kneading was the best part, pure therapy.

Challah

1 package active dry yeast
2 tablespoons sugar
5 cups all-purpose flour, spooned into cup to measure
2 teaspoons salt
1½ cups very warm water
2 eggs
2 tablespoons vegetable oil
1 egg yolk, slightly beaten
Poppy seeds

Sprinkle yeast and sugar into ¼ cup very warm water. Let stand 5 minutes, then stir. Mix flour and salt in a large bowl. Make a well in the center of the mixture and drop in whole eggs, oil, 1¼ very warm water and the yeast mix. Work liquids into the flour. Turn out on lightly floured board and knead until smooth and elastic. Put the mixture into a bowl that you have greased with butter and turn the mixture to grease the top. Cover the bowl and let it stand in a warm place for 1 hour.

Punch down, cover the bowl again and let it rise 35 minutes or until doubled in bulk. Divide the dough into 3 equal parts. Between lightly floured hands, roll the dough into 3 ropes of even length. Braid the ropes and put on greased baking sheet. Cover and let rise 20 minutes or until light. Brush with egg yolk and sprinkle with poppy seeds. Bake in moderate oven (375ºF) for about 45 minutes. Check after 15 minutes and if the braid is very brown, cover it with a piece of foil.

For Passover, when bakers can't use regular flour, she made a variety of holiday cakes.

Passover Sponge Cake I

6 eggs separated
1 cup sugar
1 teaspoon grated orange rind
¼ cup orange juice
⅜ cup Passover cake meal
3 tablespoons sifted potato starch
⅛ teaspoon salt

Beat egg yolks and sugar until thick and lemon-colored. Add orange rind and juice.

Mix cake meal, potato starch and salt until thoroughly blended. Fold into the batter.

Beat the egg whites until stiff but not dry and fold in.

Pour into an 8 inch by 8 inch by 2 inch pan lined with white parchment paper. Bake at 350ºF for about 50 minutes, until the cake is golden brown and a cake tester stuck in the center comes out clean.

Invert at once on a rack, remove the paper and invert to another rack to cool.

Passover Sponge Cake II

9 eggs separated
1¾ cup sugar
Juice and grated rind of a lemon
⅞ cup sifted potato starch

Beat the egg yolks, sugar and the whites of 2 eggs until thick and lemon colored. Add the juice and rind of the lemon. Fold in the potato starch.

Beat the 7 remaining egg whites until stiff but not dry and fold into the batter.

Grease a 9 inch by 9 inch by 2 inch cake pan and line with white parchment paper. Pour in the batter and bake at 350ºF for about 50 minutes, until well browned.

Invert on a rack, remove paper and invert to another rack to cool.

Passover Walnut Cake

9 eggs separated
½ pound extra fine sugar
2 tablespoons Passover cake meal
1/16 teaspoon salt
½ pound fine ground walnut meats

Beat the egg yolks and sugar until thick and lemon colored. Fold in the cake meal, salt and nuts. Beat the egg whites until stiff but not dry and fold in. Bake at 350ºF in a greased and parchment paper-lined 9 inch by 9 inch by 2 inch pan for 45 minutes or in a greased 9 inch tube pan for 1 hour, until cake is golden brown. Invert on rack, remove paper, invert again to another rack and cool.

Another Passover staple was matzah balls for soup. When I was young, they were hard. After my younger brother Mike married Ellen, she shared her family's tip of adding carbonated soda water to make them light.

Fluffy Matzah Balls

4 large eggs
2 tablespoon chicken fat or vegetable oil
½ cup seltzer or club soda
1 cup matzah meal
Salt and pepper to taste

Mix the eggs well with a fork. Add the chicken fat or oil, soda water, matzah meal and salt and pepper. Mix well. Cover and refrigerate for several hours.

Dip your hands in cold water and make about 10 balls slightly smaller than Ping-Pong™ balls.

Bring water to boil in a large pot. Add salt and place the matzah balls in the water. Cover and simmer about 30 minutes or until soft.

You can make ahead and add to warm soup and freeze. The liquid keeps them fluffy. Defrost the soup, reheat and serve. If you do like them harder, use large eggs and cook a shorter time.

Baking was a special love, one I inherited from Jo and passed along to my son, Daniel, who married Jenn, who has been and could again be a professional baker. Jo would willing bake at any excuse.

After my mother's sister, Evelyn, and her husband, Lee, moved near us in New Jersey, my younger cousin Barbara was a frequent overnight guest at my house. I was 11 years older than Barbara and looked upon her as my private play toy, my baby to play with, enjoy and take everywhere. I loved her dearly, except first thing in the morning when she would wake at dawn and want me to get up and bake cookies with her.

"Go get the pans ready," I'd tell her as soon as she was old enough to understand. She would dutifully get out cookie sheets and come back to report to me. "Get the flour," I'd tell her.

By this time, her rummaging around in the kitchen would have awakened Jo, who would then bake with Barbara. Cookies at 6:00 am, followed by pancakes or blintzes for breakfast. They tried all different kinds but the most common were press cookies or cut cookies in various shapes, deftly decorated by a toddler.

Basic Press Cookies

1 cup shortening
¾ cup sugar
1 egg
1 teaspoon almond extract
2½ cups sifted all-purpose flour
¼ teaspoon baking powder
¼ teaspoon salt

Preheat oven to 375ºF.

Cream shortening and sugar well. Beat in egg and almond extract. Sift flour, baking powder and salt. Gradually blend in dry ingredients. Fill cookie press and form cookies on ungreased cooking sheet. Bake 10 to 12 minutes. Remove to cooling rack. Yields 6 to 7 dozen.

If desired, add food coloring when blending ingredients.

Orange Crisps (Press Cookies)

1 cup shortening
½ cup sugar
½ cup brown sugar
1 tablespoon orange juice
1 teaspoon grated orange rind
1 egg
2½ cups sifted all-purpose flour
¼ teaspoon baking soda
¼ teaspoon salt

Preheat oven to 375ºF.

Cream shortening and sugars well. Add orange juice and grated orange rind. Beat in egg.

Sift flour, baking soda and salt. Gradually blend in dry ingredients. Fill cookie press. Form cookies on ungreased cookie sheet. Bake for 10 to 12 minutes. Remove to cooling racks. Yields 6 to 7 dozen.

Chocolate Spritz Press Cookies

½ cup shortening
1 cup sugar
1 egg
2 tablespoons milk
2 squares (2 ounces) unsweetened chocolate, melted and cooled
2 cups sifted all-purpose flour
¼ teaspoon salt

Preheat oven to 375ºF.

Cream shortening and sugar well. Beat in egg and milk. Stir in melted, cooled chocolate. Sift flour and salt. Blend in dry ingredients. Fill cookie press. Form cookies on ungreased cookie sheets. Bake 8 to10 minutes. Remove to cooling racks. Yields 3 to 4 dozen.

In addition to cooking, Jo loved gardening. When we were small, my father had built a grape arbor. Jo picked grapes and tried unsuccessfully to make wine. More successful was the sour cherry tree in our back yard that eventually yielded plenty of cherries. Of course, that meant pie.

Sour-Cherry Pie

Make a standard pastry crust for 2 crust pie. (See next recipe.)

Filling:
1 cup sugar
⅓ cup all-purpose four
⅛ teaspoon salt
4 cups freshly pitted sour cherries
¼ teaspoon almond extract
2 tablespoons butter or margarine
1 egg yolk
1 tablespoon water

Preheat oven to 400ºF. Make pastry using standard pastry crust recipe. Wrap in waxed paper and refrigerate until ready to use.

Roll out half of pastry on a lightly floured surface, creating an 11-inch circle. Fit into a 9-inch pie plate, trim.

In a large bowl, mix sugar, flour and salt. Add cherries and almond extract. Toss lightly to combine.

Turn cherry mix into pastry-lined pie plate, mounding. Dot with butter or margarine.

Roll out remaining pastry into an 11 inch circle. Make several slits near the center for steam vents. Adjust over the filling, fold edge of top crust under bottom crust, press together and crimp decoratively.

Beat egg yolk with water and brush lightly over top crust.

Bake 45 minutes until juices start to bubble through the steam vents and crust is golden brown.

Cool on wire rack for at least 1 hour. Serve slightly warm. It is especially good with vanilla ice cream.

If you need the standard pastry mix, here's a good one. Double the recipe if you are making a two crust pie.

Standard Pastry Crust

1 cup sifted all-purpose flour
½ teaspoon salt.
⅓ cup plus 1 tablespoon butter
2 tablespoons water

Mix the all-purpose flour and salt. Cut in the butter using a pastry cutter or fork. Sprinkle with the water, a few drops at a time. Mix lightly until all the dry ingredients are moistened. Press firmly into a ball and let it chill for about 10 minutes. Roll as directed for the recipe.

If your recipe calls for a pre-baked crust, roll the pastry ⅛ inch thick. Fit it into a pie pan, flute the edges and prick with a fork. Bake the crust in a preheated 450ºF oven for about 10 to 12 minutes.

If you are wondering about the grapes, here is what Jo made instead of wine.

Grape Pie

Pastry for 2 crust pie
3 cups stemmed Concord grapes
¾ cup sugar
1 tablespoon all-purpose flour
⅛ teaspoon ground cinnamon
Grated rind of 1 lemon
1 egg, well-beaten.

Separate the skins from the pulp of the grapes. Place pulp in a saucepan and cook over medium heat until seeds are free. Rub through a sieve. Cool.

Add grape skins, sugar, cinnamon, lemon rind and egg. Mix thoroughly, divide pastry and fit bottom crust into 8-inch pie plate. Pour in grape filling. Make lattice strips of remaining pastry and place over filling. Press edges together. Bake at 425ºF about 50 minutes, until golden brown. Serve hot or cold.

Jo loved going into our suburban yard and finding natural foods. Dandelions, she maintained, were an unappreciated vegetable. She would add the leaves to salads and use them in cooking, along with wild chives she unearthed.

Dandelion Omelet

¼ cup unopened dandelion buds
¼ cup chopped sweet red peppers
2 tablespoons margarine or butter, divided
4 eggs
½ teaspoon water
½ cup shredded cheddar cheese.
Dandelion blossoms

In an 8-inch nonstick skillet, over medium heat, sauté dandelion buds and red peppers in 1 tablespoon butter or margarine for 2 to 3 minutes. Remove and set aside. In the same skillet, melt remaining butter or margarine. In a small bowl, beat the eggs and water. Pour into the skillet, cook over medium heat. As eggs set, lift edges, letting uncooked portion flow underneath. When eggs are set, sprinkle with cheese. Spoon dandelion mix over half the eggs. Fold omelet in half. Garnish with dandelion blossoms. Yields 2 servings.

Here's an alternative when you don't have dandelions.

Omelette Elegante

1 egg
⅓ cup whipped cottage cheese
4 ounces canned sliced mushrooms
1 tablespoon sliced pimento
½ teaspoon dried onion
Salt and pepper to taste

Beat egg and whipped cottage cheese thoroughly together. Add other ingredients and mix thoroughly. Put in buttered or Teflon pan and cook about 3 to 4 minutes.

Although cooking was always important to Jo, it was put on a lower flame while my brothers and I were growing up. She regularly baked for Parent Teacher Association (PTA) events, where she served as President, and for charity bake sales. She worked in the television repair store, as we all did at some point. Yet, with three children to raise, there was little time left for other than daily cooking to get meals on the table.

Yet, a dream remained. As my brothers and I grew up, Jo stoically worked on her cooking whenever she could, voicing a wish of someday pursuing it in some professional manner. My brothers, Karl and Michael, and I paid little attention to her passion, except to eat the results. We went off to college and then married and began families of our own.

My father, Al, worked in the store and taught electronics at Bergan Technical School, a local community college. Then, more and more, he gravitated toward teaching and decided to return to school to get his teaching degree. He was accepted at Montclair State Teacher's College and took night classes to earn his degree. He secured a job as an Industrial Arts Teacher in Monmouth High School, many miles away, and regularly made the long trip to the school and back. It was grueling but he loved it and his students loved him.

Jo and Al were saving for retirement and had plans to move into the small efficiency apartment my dad had fashioned in the Lake George cabin. They would put their plan into effect to rent out the lower cabin, a main room, porch and two bedrooms, while living in the efficiency located over the bedrooms.

It never happened. First Al developed diabetes. Then he was very tired, then jaundiced. Test after test yielded nothing, until it was too late and it was discovered he had pancreatic cancer. It was a death sentence in the 1970s and little has changed since then. He died in the hospital in January 1974, just after his 60th birthday.

It soon became apparent that Jo, deep in mourning, could not support both the house in Saddle Brook and the cabin on Lake George. I was pregnant with my second child at the time. My first child, Alisa, having been born in 1971. My husband and I invited Jo to live with us in an arrangement where we supported her and she watched our children while we worked. She agreed but confessed that she had always wanted to go to school, to college. Could she somehow manage that?

The answer was a resounding "Yes!." Pace University was within easy driving distance. In a still-grieving flurry of activity in May 1974, Jo sold the Saddle Brook house, my husband and I sold our small house and we moved into a larger home with room for all of us, my family of four, Jo and even my grandmother Ray staying with us for a while. Jo threw herself into helping my family. My kids never lacked for interesting meals and learned to eat a large variety of foods. One special recipe they liked was this one that they could play with and then eat, as long as their hands were scrubbed clean.

Peanut Butter Playdough

1 cup peanut butter
1 cup white corn syrup
1 cup powdered sugar
3 cups powdered milk

Mix together, play and eat!

Jo blossomed at Pace University. She tackled all the reading, papers and reports with gusto. As a girl, Jo had been accepted to college after high school but quit after six months to marry and then support my dad going to college. They could only afford one education. For years my dad had told my mother she didn't need college. She took this to mean she was too "dumb" for the classes. Now, after a few weeks in class she realized he might have meant something different: her life experience was a university.

She was an outstanding student at Pace, where she studied business marketing and nurtured her dream: One day, she would open her own food business, where she would make items from scratch. One day.

Over the next few years, Jo watched my children during the day and attended college in the evenings. Then, when my brother and sister-in-law needed childcare, we added two more children to her load. It had to be hard. Each day, Alison and Marc would be dropped off at my house by my sister-in-law, Ellen, who was a teacher. I would give the four children, Alisa, Dan, Alison and Marc, breakfast, turn them over to Jo and head out to work. In the afternoons, Ellen would get to the house from school about 4 pm, freeing Jo to go to class. I would arrive about 5 pm since my job ended at 4:30 pm.

No matter how busy she was, Jo still found time to cook. The kids loved this recipe and would make funny faces with the batter.

Funnel Cakes

For 30 cakes

3 eggs well-beaten
2 cups milk
4 cups sifted all-purpose flour
⅓ cup sugar
½ teaspoon salt
1 tablespoon baking powder
Fat or oil for deep frying
Confectioners' sugar

For 10 cakes

1 egg well beaten
⅔ cup milk
1⅓ cups sifted all-purpose flour
⅑ cup sugar
dash of salt
⅓ tablespoon baking powder
Fat or oil for deep frying
Confectioners' sugar

Beat eggs with milk and gradually beat in flour, sugar, salt and baking powder. Beat until very smooth.

Holding the opening of a funnel closed, fill the funnel with the batter. Open the end of the funnel and allow dough to run out in a stream into deep hot fat (375ºF on a frying thermometer). Move the funnel to make a pattern starting at the center of the pan and swirling batter outward in a circle.

Fry for 2 or 3 minutes, or until golden brown. Drain on absorbent paper and sprinkle with confectioners' sugar.

In contrast to the funnel cakes, these recipes counted as healthy.

Raisin Nut Strudel

4 cups unsifted all-purpose four
3 teaspoons baking powder
½ teaspoon salt
Sugar
½ cup vegetable oil
¼ cup butter or margarine melted
¼ cup orange juice
1 teaspoon vanilla
3 eggs
⅓ cup tart jelly (cherry or other flavor)
1 cut soft white raisins
1 cup chopped nuts
12 maraschino cherries, diced
1 teaspoon cinnamon
1 egg white, slightly beaten

Sift flour, baking powder, salt and ¾ cup sugar into a bowl.

Make a well in the center and add oil, butter or margarine, orange juice, vanilla and eggs.

Mix to form a soft dough. Knead a few times on floured board to form a smooth dough. Cut into four even pieces. Roll each to form a circle about ¼ inch thick.

Spread each with a thin coat of jelly. Sprinkle with raisins, nuts and cherries.

Mix ½ cup sugar and cinnamon and sprinkle some lightly over fruits and nuts.

Roll tightly and put on greased cookie sheet. Prick with fork and brush with egg white.

Sprinkle remaining cinnamon-sugar mix.

Bake in moderate oven at 350ºF for 45 minutes, until golden brown.

Cool, cut in slices. Can be wrapped in foil and frozen.

Simple Apple Strudel

2 apples, peeled, sliced and cored
¼ cup sugar
¼ cup raisins
2 tablespoons chopped nuts
½ teaspoon cinnamon
Rind of 1 lemon
¼ cup butter
¼ cup dry breadcrumbs
Confectioners' sugar
Filo dough (Jo sometimes made her own dough, but using prepared is much easier)

Preheat oven to 375ºF. Combine apples with the sugar, raisins, nuts, cinnamon and lemon rind and put aside.

Take out filo sheet and spread on a board. Brush the filo sheet with melted butter and sprinkle with 1 tablespoon of breadcrumbs.

Place a second sheet of filo on top of the first. Brush this with butter and sprinkle with breadcrumbs.

Place some of the apple mixture at the end of the filo sheets, leaving a 1 inch border. Fold the sides in 1 inch.

Starting at the end, carefully roll, jelly-roll style, ending with the seam on the bottom. Brush the top with more butter.

Place the roll on a parchment paper.

Bake for 35 minutes, until golden brown.

Fat-free Banana Bread

Oil for greasing pan
2½ cups cake flour
2 teaspoons baking powder
1 teaspoon baking soda
1 teaspoon ground cinnamon
½ cup applesauce
1 cup granulated sugar
1½ cups egg whites
2 cups very ripe bananas peeled and mashed (about 6 medium bananas)
1 teaspoon vanilla extract

Preheat oven to 350ºF. Lightly grease a 9 inch by 5 inch loaf pan with oil, butter or cooking spray.

Combine flour, baking powder, baking soda and cinnamon.

Whisk together applesauce, sugar, egg whites, bananas and vanilla. Add flour mix all at once and stir gently to blend. Do not overbeat.

Pour batter into prepared loaf pan and bake 45 to 50 minutes or until knife inserted in center comes out clean.

Cool completely before slicing. 16 servings.

Fat-free Carrot Cake

2 cups cake flour
2 teaspoons baking powder
1 teaspoon baking soda
1 teaspoon ground cinnamon
½ teaspoon salt
1 cup applesauce
1 cup light brown sugar
1 cup granulated sugar
3 egg whites
Grated rind and juice of one orange
1 cup peeled, shredded carrots
1 cup raisins
Orange glaze (see next page)

Preheat oven to 350ºF. Lightly grease a Bundt-style pan or 10-inch spring form pan with center hole.

Combine flour, baking powder, baking soda, cinnamon and salt, set aside.

Beat together applesauce, sugars, egg whites, orange rind and juice. Blend in flour mixture with mixer at medium speed, beating only until smooth. Do not overbeat. Stir in carrots and raisins.

Pour batter into prepared pan and bake 50 to 60 minutes or until a knife inserted near the center comes out clean. Remove cake from pan. If using spring form pan, removes sides of pan and put cake on wire rack to cool completely. Spoon orange glaze over cake and serve. Yields 20 servings.

Orange glaze

2 cups confectioners' sugar
4 tablespoons orange juice
1 tablespoon lemon juice
1 teaspoon grated orange rind

Combine ingredients and stir thoroughly to blend.

Yields enough glaze for one cake.

After a few years, I changed jobs and needed more education. I began a Master of Business Administration (MBA) degree program and with Jo and my husband, who was attending an Executive MBA program on weekends and alternate Fridays, we juggled child care, meals and life.

Jo earned excellent grades and completely enjoyed the academic environment. She created a business plan for a small catering company and cooked so much, on paper at least, that she became wealthy—on paper.

We graduated together in 1981 in a memorable ceremony at Avery Fisher Hall at Lincoln Center, New York City.

Jo immediately set to work planning specific recipes she would use in her business. Baked goods would be the centerpiece.

Applesauce Raisin Cookies

2 cups flour
½ teaspoon baking powder
½ teaspoon baking soda
½ teaspoon ground cinnamon
¼ teaspoon ground allspice
¼ teaspoon salt
½ cup margarine, softened
½ cup granulated sugar
¼ cup packed brown sugar
1 large egg
1 cup unsweetened applesauce
1 teaspoon vanilla
1 medium Granny Smith apple, finely chopped
1 cup coarsely chopped walnuts
1 cup dark raisins

Lemon Glaze

1 cup confectioners' sugar
2 tablespoons fresh lemon juice

Preheat oven to 375ºF.

Grease 2 large cookie sheets.

In a medium bowl, combine flour, baking powder, baking soda, allspice and salt.

In a large mixing bowl, with mixer at medium speed, beat margarine and sugars until light and fluffy. Reduce speed to low; beat in egg,

applesauce and vanilla until well-blended. Add dry ingredients a little at a time until the entire mixture is blended. With a spoon, stir in the apples.

Drop dough by rounded measuring tablespoon, 1 inch apart on prepared cookie sheet. Bake cookies on two oven racks for 20 to 22 minutes or until slightly browned around the edges and set, rotating the cookie sheets between upper and low racks half way through baking time.

While cookies bake, prepare Lemon Glaze.

In a small bowl, stir confectioners' sugar and lemon juice until smooth.

Transfer baked cookies to wire rack.

With pastry brush, smooth the glaze over the warm cookies, cool completely.

But where to run her business?

The Lake George cabin was her location of choice. We discussed turning the cabin into a kitchen but that left no room for living. The existing kitchen was still the tiny affair it had always been.

Right down the hill was an alternative. There was a tiny building that had once served as a gas service station but now was abandoned. It was white clapboard, about 12 feet by 12 feet, with a gravel parking area in front. The gas pumps were gone. It was now used for storage.

Jo was faced with a choice. The kitchen at the cabin was very outdated and small. She could use funds to build a new kitchen or to open a business. It was a no-brainer for her. She wanted the business.

And so she approached the nearby neighbor who owned the small building. He was willing to rent it to her for a minimum amount, providing she did all the fixing up herself.

Jo jumped at the chance. That summer the entire family cleaned, scrapped, painted, re-roofed and furbished the tiny outlet with used restaurant equipment: freezer, glass door cooler, six burner oven, refrigerator, industrial sized mixer, microwave, wire racks and whatever else Jo sourced.

Next, she purchased industrial-sized containers of spices, herbs and other ingredients.

In the summer of 1981, the business was registered as "Herbs and Spices" to suggest the cooking from scratch goal, and Jo opened her doors. Business boomed. Neighbors were soon stopping in regularly. Tourists stopped since it was the first and only food place after making the long trek over the mountain on Route 9N. Local workers in the nearby guest houses and marina came for sandwiches. Jo was so busy she could not keep up with the flood of people.

Her routine was to wake up at 4 am and begin baking. She made breads, muffins, pies, cakes, rolls and her soon-to-become famous chocolate chip cookies and rugelach. Most things sold out the same day and customers began ordering items for the weekend to make sure she would have enough for them. Her prices were very reasonable—perhaps too reasonable—but her love was to feed people, not fleece them.

After her baking was done, she made fresh sandwiches for lunch and would cook new items for dinners. She would create individual portions and freeze them so customers could have quick gourmet dinners. This was no fast-food restaurant. Jo would multiply recipes such as this relatively easy one.

Stuffed Miniature Eggplants

2 (6 ounce) small oriental eggplants
1 small zucchini, grated
1 small red bell pepper, chopped
1 green onion, thinly sliced
1½ teaspoons dried oregano leaf
1 tablespoon olive oil
Salt and pepper to taste

Wash eggplants and cut off caps. Cut into halves lengthwise. Arrange eggplants cut side down in a baking dish, cover with plastic wrap. Rotating dish midway through cooking, microwave on high 4½ to 5 minutes. Let stand.

Put zucchini, bell pepper, onion and oregano into a 4-cup glass measuring cup. Cover with plastic wrap and microwave on high 2 to 3 minutes; drain. Scoop pulp from cooked eggplant and return hollowed shells to baking dish. Coarsely chop pulp and add zucchini mix. Add olive oil and salt and pepper to taste. Mound mix into eggplant shells. Cover and microwave on high for 2 minutes. Makes 4 miniature eggplants.

It had to be a family affair. My sister-in-law Ellen and I often found ourselves in the store, waiting on customers, cleaning, making sandwiches or microwaving orders. This was not something we yearned to do, after all we were on vacation. I held a full time job with limited vacation periods. Ellen was a teacher who dreamed of having her summers off. However, we saw Jo struggling to keep up with the many customers and couldn't desert her. She hired a helper but even that was not enough and the girl did not work nearly half as hard as Ellen and I did or even a quarter as hard as Jo.

I think one of the most satisfying moments in the too-brief history of "Herbs and Spices" took place in California. My brother Mike was on a trip and was introduced to some people at a social event. Conversation turned to travel and vacations and Mike mentioned his family had a house on Lake George in New York State. "Lake George!" exclaimed his new acquaintance. "Let me tell you about a great place there that you wouldn't believe." The acquaintance proceeded to describe the "best rugelach" he'd ever eaten and the tiny store where they were sold—at the bottom of the long mountain road north of Bolton Landing.

After a few minutes of listening to the narrative, Mike said something like, "I know. That's my mother's place."

When told, Jo beamed like a searchlight. Unsought praise from a stranger made it all worthwhile!

Here are her famous rugelach recipes.

Rugelach

1 cake yeast
1 cup sour cream
4 cups unsifted all-purpose flour
3 egg yolks, well-beaten
1 pound butter (or part margarine)
½ cup sugar
1/16 teaspoon salt
Jam, any flavor
Raisins
Ground Cinnamon
Sugar
Ground nut meats
Shredded coconut

Have all ingredients at room temperature. Crumble the yeast into the cream. Alternately add the flour and egg yolks. Cream together the butter, ½ cup sugar and salt and blend thoroughly into the batter. Divide the dough into 4 parts; wrap each in waxed paper and chill in the refrigerator overnight.

The next day, roll out each section of the dough into a strip 6 inches wide and ¼ inch thick. Spread each with jam and sprinkle with any or all of the following: raisins, ground cinnamon, sugar, ground nut meats and shredded coconut.

Roll up and cut each roll into 12 slices.

Place on greased cookie sheets and bake at 375ºF about 30 minutes, until a golden brown.

Chocolate Rugelach

2 sticks (1 cup) unsalted butter softened
1 brick (8 ounces) cream cheese, softened
¼ cup granulated sugar
2 cups all-purpose flour
⅓ cup fig preserves
1½ cups sweetened shredded coconut
½ cup semi-sweet chocolate bits
4 tablespoons sugar

Decoration: white coarse crystal sugar

Pastry: beat butter and cream cheese using an electric mixer in a large bowl on medium speed until well-combined.

Divide the dough in four pieces. Shape each portion into a 1-inch thick disc. Wrap individually and refrigerate at least 4 hours until firm enough to roll out.

Heat oven to 350ºF. Place oven rack in upper third of oven.

Melt preserves in microwave or a saucepan over low heat (strain if chunky).

On floured surface, roll each disc into a 10-inch circle. Brush with a quarter of the preserves. It will barely cover the dough. Sprinkle with coconut, 2 tablespoons chocolate bits and 1 tablespoon granulated sugar. Gently press so filling adheres to dough. With a pizza wheel or knife, cut the circles into 12 pie form wedges.

Roll up each wedge from end to point. Place 2 inches apart on ungreased baking sheet. Sprinkle wedges with coarse sugar.

Bake in upper third of oven 18 to 22 minutes or until golden brown.

Remove to wire rack to cool.

Repeat with the remaining dough and filling.

Makes 48 pieces.

Brownies, pies, cakes, apple strudel and even homemade doughnuts came out of "Herbs and Spices" on a regular basis. The business boomed.

Doughnuts

3 eggs slightly beaten
10 ounces sugar
1½ ounces fat (shortening or unsalted butter), melted and cooled
1 pound 10 ounces flour
1 teaspoon nutmeg
1¼ teaspoons salt
⅛ teaspoon ginger
3 tablespoons baking powder
2 teaspoons grated orange rind
1 pint milk
Confectioners' or granulated sugar.

Preheat deep fat fryer filled with liquid vegetable oil to 350ºF to 375ºF.

Mix eggs, sugar and shortening or butter at medium speed on mixer for about 10 minutes.

Add combined dry ingredients, alternating with milk.

Mix to form a soft dough. Add more flour if dough is too soft to handle.

Chill, roll into ⅜ inch thickness on floured board.

Cut with 2½ inch round cutter.

Fry in deep fat fryer for 3 to 4 minutes.

Sprinkle with confectioners' or granulated sugar when partly cool.

Can top with melted chocolate or other icing for variety.

Yields 4 dozen.

Instead of ice cream, Jo offered frozen bananas and they went quickly.

Frozen Banana Pops

8 bananas, peeled
8 craft sticks
32 ounces semi-sweet chocolate chopped or chips

Optional toppings: nuts, granola, sprinkles, crispy rice cereal

Lay out waxed paper on a baking sheet.

Cut the bananas in half (top and bottom, not lengthwise) and insert a craft stick into each.

Freeze for an hour or more, until hard.

When frozen, melt the chocolate in a double-boiler or in the microwave in a microwave proof measuring cup, checking it every 30 seconds or less until melted.

Roll or dip each half of banana in the melted chocolate.

If desired, immediately roll in the toppings.

Freeze until the chocolate sets, about 30 minutes.

Wrap each in plastic wrap for individual servings.

Save up to a week.

Jo kept the business going for three summers: three hard work summers for the entire family. With each passing year, she lost money. The issue wasn't a lack of interest. In the summer, the place was packed at breakfast and lunch, with a healthy smattering of business for dinner. Plus, she had standing weekly orders for her baked goods and the summer crowd began to ask her to provide take-out meals for catering.

The problem was that the day after Labor Day the summer crowd started to pack up and go home and two weeks into September only the few permanent residents and the marina workers remained. But the overhead, especially insurance for a business, was year-round. Even with a generous reduction of her rent from her understanding landlord, the business was doomed.

As she watched her small bank balance disappear, Jo had to admit defeat. She reluctantly closed the business and returned to family cooking. Her "Herbs and Spices" sign was taken down and was stored in the shed.

Her downtime didn't last long. Jo was now living at the lake cottage in the summer and with her children during the rest of the year. She went from living with me, Elaine, to living with her oldest son, Karl, who had a new daughter. Jo helped with baby Andrea, until she was called again in 1986 to live with youngest son, Micheal, and his wife Ellen. They had been blessed with a surprise baby, Joshua, and moved to Niskayuna, in the Albany, New York area, where Mike had a new job.

Meanwhile, the family chipped in to build a new, big kitchen at the cabin, using the "Herbs and Spices" sign as part of the floor underlay. Jo filled the new country kitchen with every pot, pan, utensil and gadget that can be imagined. As time went on, the refrigerators got bigger and bigger.

Jo liked to make things from scratch that most people would go out and buy. It was the challenge that excited her.

Baba Ganoush

1 large eggplant, unpeeled
½ cup pine nuts or pecans, toasted
¼ cup finely chopped fresh parsley
3 tablespoons tahini (sesame paste)
3 tablespoons fresh lemon juice
1 garlic clove, minced and mashed into a paste with a pinch of salt

Preheat oven to 400ºF with rack in center of oven.

Prick the eggplant a few times with a fork and place on baking sheet. Bake until the eggplant collapses, about 40 minutes. Cool until the eggplant can be handled.

Scrape the flesh off the eggplant's skin into a food processor. Discard skin. Add nuts, parsley, tahini, lemon juice, garlic paste and salt to taste. Process until smooth. Serve immediately or cover and refrigerate for up to 3 days. Great with crackers as an appetizer.

Jo enjoyed being needed and continued to enjoy cooking. When she moved to Mike and Ellen's home, she became actively involved in the Jewish temple, Congregation Gates of Heaven. She was a member of the sisterhood, the book club, torah study and many temple activities. At one point, she made her acting debut in a small part in the temple production of "Fiddler on the Roof." If there was an event, she manned a booth and contributed anything that was needed. She made hundreds of fabric cherries for the Cherry Blossom Festival fundraiser and contributed food on each and every occasion.

Often the more complex the recipe, the better she liked it.

Mandelbrot

Two bakings are required. Do the first baking a day or so ahead and the final baking shortly before serving.

3 eggs
1 cup sugar
½ cup vegetable oil
1 teaspoon almond or vanilla extract
2 tablespoons orange juice
1 tablespoon grated fresh orange rind
1 teaspoon grated fresh lemon rind
3 cups flour
¼ teaspoon salt
3 teaspoons baking powder
2 cups slivered almonds
1 teaspoon cinnamon
1 tablespoon sugar

In a large mixing bowl, beat eggs until thick and lemon-colored. Add sugar gradually, beating constantly. Add oil while continuing to beat. Mix in extract, orange juice, orange and lemon rinds.

Sift together flour, salt and baking powder, then mix with almonds. Add to egg and sugar mix about ⅓ at a time, mixing well.

For easier handling chill dough several hours or overnight.

Turn out dough to a well-floured board, dip your hands in flour, then knead dough about a dozen turns.

Divide dough into 2 or 3 pieces and pat each into strips about 3 inches wide by 1 inch thick and about 10 inches to 12 inches long.

Place strips on well-oiled and floured shallow baking pan (10½ by 15½ by 2 inches is a good size).

Bake at 350ºF for 40 to 45 minutes or until golden brown.

Remove at once to board and, while still warm, cut with a serrated knife into ½ inch slices.

Let slices cool.

Rearrange slices in baking pan, turning on their sides. Sprinkle with mix of cinnamon and sugar and bake at 400ºF until light browned.

Yields 5 dozen.

Jo enjoyed getting into her work.

Thumbprint Cookies

1½ cups all-purpose flour
1 teaspoon baking soda
¼ teaspoon salt
⅔ cups sugar
¼ cup butter (or margarine), softened
1 egg white
1 teaspoon vanilla
½ cup no-sugar added raspberry or apricot fruit spread

Combine flour, baking soda and salt in medium bowl; set aside.

Beat sugar, butter, egg white and vanilla in large bowl until blended, using an electric mixer at high speed.

Add flour mixture, mix well.

Press mixture together to form a ball.

Refrigerate 30 minutes.

Preheat oven to 375ºF. Lightly coat cookie sheet with nonstick cooking spray.

Shape dough in 1 inch balls with lightly floured hands. Place on cookie sheet. Press down with thumb in center of each ball to form a small well.

Bake 10 to 12 minutes or until golden brown. Remove to wire rack and cool. Fill each well with about 1 teaspoon fruit spread.

One of her most famous recipes was for Hamantaschen, cookies for Purim. These three-cornered hat-shaped cookies celebrate the victory of the Jewish people over the villain, Haman. Jo would bake hundreds with the temple youth group.

Hamantaschen

2 cups sifted all-purpose flour
1½ teaspoon double-acting baking powder
⅜ cup sugar
$\frac{1}{16}$ teaspoon salt
2 eggs well beaten
3 tablespoons salad oil
Grated rind of a lemon or orange
Orange juice to soften dough enough to be able to roll dough easily on floured board

Sift flour, baking powder, sugar and salt together. Add eggs, oil and rind. Mix to a dough. Add orange juice only to ease kneading. Roll out on a floured board to ⅛ inch thickness and cut into 4-inch circles. Place a spoonful of any filling in the center of the circle and bring up sides to form a 3 cornered triangle, with the filling peeking through the middle. Press edges securely together.

Bake on cookie sheet at 375ºF for about 20 minutes, until light brown.

Yields about 2 dozen.

Suggested Fillings

Traditionally, Hamantaschen are filled with poppy seed fillings but may be filled with any fillings you can find or make, such as apricot, raspberry, blueberry, strawberry, cherry, which are readily available in most supermarkets or on-line.

Poppy Seed Filling

1 cup poppy seeds
1 egg yolk
2 tablespoons fresh lemon juice
3 tablespoons finely chopped nuts

Mix all ingredients, blending well.

Jo contributed to the temple cookbook. She even filmed a segment for cable television on Jewish Cooking. This was her element. If only she'd been discovered; perhaps she could have rivaled Julia Child!.

As Joshua grew and went to school, Jo increased her volunteer activities. She volunteered at Daughters of Sarah Nursing Home and taught in the English as a Second Language program. Her volunteer work was honored by B'nai B'rith with a Volunteer Award.

She loved life and filled it with big and small pleasures, including family, some travel and the little things. Here, in her own words, is a document she wrote about things she loved.

Twenty-One Things I Love to Do

1. To walk in the woods in the different seasons.
2. To drink the icy waters from the falls in the hills.
3. To paddle a canoe on the still waters of a lake.
4. To garden indoors and outdoors.
5. To weave on a hand loom.
6. To crochet and create items.
7. To cook intricate or interesting foods.
8. To watch people around me grow and learn.
9. To learn new things.
10. To write, mainly essay type papers.
11. To listen to my mother tell of her youth.
12. To read, mainly history and biography.
13. To sew by hand, examples, dolls, quilts.
14. To remember.
15. To listen to WQXR when doing most of above.
16. To sleep in a hammock under a tree.
17. To eat.
18. To hope and strive with others for a better world.
19. To watch a good play put on by sincere players.
20. To make articles out of wood: sawing, hammering, sanding.
21. To do Sunday Times crossword.

A few years after the turn of the century, Jo's health began to fail. First, just a little as her memory wasn't what it once was and her taste buds disappeared. Then came 2003 and the tragic death of granddaughter, Alison, who was lost to a fast-growing cancer. Jo experienced a series of mini strokes, TIA (transient ischemic attacks). Eventually, she began to lose functioning and in 2005, refusing to be what she called a "burden to her children," she made the decision to enter a nursing home.

She was admitted to Daughters of Sarah into the Memory Unit and continued to do whatever she could to enjoy life. Her children regularly took her on outings and continued to take her to the cabin at Lake George.

One of the last times she had the chance to be in her Lake George cabin kitchen and cook was with me, when together we made Jo's Famous Chocolate Chip Cookies. Here is the recipe and a poem I wrote about this moment that will forever be in my memory.

Chocolate Chip Cookies

1⅛ cups flour
¼ teaspoon baking soda
½ teaspoon salt
½ cup butter or shortening
¼ cup brown sugar
½ cup granulated sugar
1 egg beaten
1 teaspoon vanilla
½ package (6 ounces) semi-sweet chocolate bits

Sift flour, baking soda and salt together.

In an electric mixer, cream shortening and brown sugar and granulated sugar together.

Add egg and vanilla. Beat thoroughly.

Add sifted dry ingredients a little at a time. Blend thoroughly.

Fold in chocolate bits.

Drop by teaspoon onto cookie sheet.

Bake in moderate 350ºF oven for about 10 minutes.

Cookies should be underdone for best results.

Baking Cookies with Momma

By Elaine Auerbach

1950

I'm five years old and I can bake cookies
With Momma.
She lets me measure the flour
But she pours it in the mixer
Because that's dangerous.
She adds the sugar that I helped measure.
I mix in the chocolate chips and don't eat many.
Then I drop big balls of batter on the cookie sheet.
"Make them smaller," says Momma. But
I'm making the biggest cookie in the world,
The biggest cookie to last my lifetime.

2005

I'm baking cookies again, with Momma.
She measures the flour
But I pour it in the mixer
Because that's dangerous.
I add the sugar because she's forgotten it.
She mixes in the chocolate chips and can't eat any,
Then she drops big balls of batter on the cookie sheet.
"Make them smaller," I tell Momma. But
she's making the biggest cookie in the world.
The biggest cookie to last her lifetime.

Jo passed away December 5, 2009, just two weeks before her 90th birthday. We'd been teasing her that we planned on having a big party for her. She was losing the ability to speak but still managed to tell us she "didn't want a party." She was lost to the world most of the time, but could still recognize photos of family and family members who visited her. Not long before she died, a family member she hadn't seen in years stopped by to visit her at the nursing home, expecting her not to remember him. To his surprise, as he walked into the room she said gaily "Hi Dave!"

People and cooking: that was Jo. That was her form of love.

Index of Recipes

ABOUT THE AUTHOR

Elaine Auerbach is Jo's daughter. Elaine's career includes writing briefly for The Patterson Evening News, Patterson, New Jersey, then serving as Associate Editor of Reader's Digest for 13 years. She next moved to PepsiCo, Inc., where she spent three decades handling a variety of internal and external communications, ultimately becoming Director of External Affairs, responsible for external communications, including corporate reports and publications, press releases, the corporate web site, corporate event literature and creating presentations and videos. Elaine has received many awards for her communications work at PepsiCo.

Elaine is the author of the critically acclaimed book, "**Fairy Tales for Women Who Have Been Through the Mill**," available on Amazon and Kindle books. She is currently working on a book of poetry and a memoir of her travels throughout the world.

Email Elaine at <u>fairytalesforwomen@gmail.com</u>

41443897R00070

Made in the USA
Middletown, DE
12 March 2017